LOOKING BACK AT
Withington & Didsbury

Gay Sussex · Peter Helm

Willow PUBLISHING

Willow Publishing

Willow Cottage, 36 Moss Lane,
Timperley, Altrincham,
Cheshire, WA15 6SZ

© Peter Helm 1988
© Gay Sussex 1988

ISBN 0 946361 25 8

Printed by The Commercial
Centre Ltd., Hollinwood,
Oldham.

Contents

Foreword

Gay Sussex and Peter Helm have worked together researching and writing the histories of a number of suburbs of Manchester — Longsight, Rusholme, Fallowfield, Levenshulme and Burnage. Some of these areas share borders with Withington and Didsbury, and it was often frustrating to exclude an item of particular historical interest because it lay over the border. So it was with real enthusiasm that they approached work on Withington and Didsbury; the links with the areas they had already covered made a satisfying whole. The original Manor of Withington had included what became the townships of Withington, Didsbury, Burnage, Rusholme and Levenshulme (as well as Chorlton-cum-Hardy, Moss Side, Denton, and Haughton), so it is not surprising that there are so many connections and similarities between the areas, which interweave to make an interesting story.

However, Didsbury and Withington do differ from these other suburbs. Their history seems longer, better documented, and more complex. A church which dates from the 13th century, a manorial system with its Court Leet, and villages which have largely withstood the developers' plans, all add to the interest.

This book is not a complete history of the area; it is a book which has been written around a collection of photographs. These photographs have been carefully chosen to illustrate many aspects of Victorian, Edwardian, and more recent life — social, religious, educational, and recreational. A historical introduction and two early maps have been included to give the photographs a context, and there is a list of books at the end of this book for those wishing to read further.

Many people have assisted with information and photographs; it would have been impossible to write this book without them. Thanks must go to Mr E France, Mrs Diana Leitch, Mrs Sue Good, The Rev N Leak, Mary Hetherington, Mrs A Middleton, Mr & Mrs Lea, Chris and Lucy Heaps, Geoff Hague, Mrs M Gregory, Mr V Smith, Joe Shabetai, Joe and Linda Goldberg, Mr C Atkinson, Vera Jackson, Carol Mitchell, Nellie Woodhall, Mrs Coralie Adamson, and Mr S Mottershead; and to Sabina Grubb who copied many of the photographs. Staff at Manchester's Local History Library, and the Photographic Department; the City Planning Department, the Documentary Photography Archive at Manchester Polytechnic, and the Police History Museum all proved, as usual, to be very kind and helpful.

This book had its origin in an appeal for old photographs organised by Robert Waterhouse in the South Manchester Reporter. Mr Waterhouse was unable to complete the project, and it was taken on by the present authors. He would like to thank all those people who were so generous in loaning their treasures, and were so patient with the inevitable delays, and hopes that they will enjoy the final publication. His thanks go to Mrs Warwick, Mrs Queenie Shalom, Mr W Fletcher, Mrs Bessie Woods, Miss E M Platt, Mrs J Malkowski, Mrs K Glyn Jones, Mr Stephen Hewitt, Mrs P Jones, Mr S Dalton, Mr E France, Mr A Stockwell, Mrs J M Seed, Mr Ian Pollitt, Mr V R Cattan, Rev Norman Leak, Miss G V Salkeld, Mrs V Johnson, Mr Loebell, Mr Baker, Ms Eileen Jones, and Mr Vincent Smith; with special thanks to Ian Pollitt, and to Ernest France, co-author of the informative book 'A New History of Didsbury', published by E J Morten in 1976.

Families generally act as important sources of help, criticism, and support in the production of a book, and the writers would like to thank Dorothy Helm, and Graham, Merida, and Jasmine Sussex who certainly did.

Gay Sussex and Peter Helm, 1988.

Introduction

Didsbury and Withington together comprise a well established area with a sense of history and continuity. Their boundaries and administration have reflected the changes in land use and local government over the years, but many of the older buildings have remained, the trees in parks and gardens are mature, and there is very little urban decay.

For the purposes of this book Withington is seen as commencing at Derby Road — *Looking Back at Rusholme and Fallowfield* travelled down Wilmslow Road to Mauldeth Road and contains a photograph of the toll bar at Mauldeth Road — and finishing at Lapwing Lane and Fog Lane. On the west it is bounded by Princess Road and on the east by Kingsway. For our purposes, Didsbury commences at Lapwing Lane and Fog Lane and takes in the area down to the River Mersey, with the same boundaries of Kingsway and Princess Road. These are rough boundaries, and certainly at various times the boundaries have been much more complicated; for example the borders with Burnage were very irregular; possibly reflecting old boundaries based on the strip farming system.

Poor Law administration had also played a part in determining the boundaries of the area we now know as Withington. The Poor Relief Act of 1662 which transferred the operation of the Poor Law from large parishes to smaller village units led to the division of the Manor of Withington into nine smaller areas — Withington, Didsbury, Burnage, Chorlton, Rusholme, Moss Side, Levenshulme, Denton and Haughton.

Although we have treated Didsbury and Withington as the two main areas, West Didsbury has some interesting features and has therefore received some attention as a separate area. West Didsbury is taken to be the area west of Palatine Road from Cavendish Road/Lapwing Lane to the River Mersey.

The arrangement of the photographs within these areas follows the line of Wilmslow Road from Withington southwards, with diversions principally along Burton Road, Palatine Road, Fog Lane, and School Lane. As Withington is reached before Didsbury journeying out of central Manchester, and as it has a historical importance as the original manor, it will be examined first.

Withington Village, c1910

Withington

The earliest mentions of Withington as a settled and identifiable area occur around the 1200's, and are in connection with families associated with the Manor of Withington. The first Lord of the Manor is believed to have been William, son of Wulfrith de Withington, in the early 1200's. The Manor covered a wide area — Withington, Didsbury, Chorlton-cum-Hardy, Moss Side, Burnage, Levenshulme, Fallowfield, Rusholme, Denton and Haughton. Later in the thirteenth century Robert Grelle (or Grelley), the Lord of the Manor of Manchester, granted Withington, which was a sub-manor of Manchester, to Matthew de Hathersage in return for one knight's fee. A knight's fee meant that if war broke out, Matthew de Hathersage could be called to bear arms for Robert Grelle.

From the end of the thirteenth century until the sixteenth century, when it passed to Sir Nicholas Mosley, the Manor was held by the Longford family. A new manor house was built for Sir Nicholas, and we can still see this house today — Hough End Hall. During the mid-eighteenth century the Egertons of Tatton became Lords of the Manor and the last Lord was the fourth Baron Egerton of Tatton who died in 1958.

Under the manorial system, tenant farmers owed obedience, loyalty, labour and some produce to the Lord of the Manor, who owned the land and was expected to see that things ran reasonably smoothly. The Manor of Withington was governed by its own court, the Court Leet, which used to meet at the Red Lion during the eighteenth and nineteenth centuries. The last meeting was held there in 1841. This forerunner of our present system of local government dealt with such problems as noise, polluted food, and stray animals, and its members were appointed by the Lord.

The origin of the name of an area can give a clue to its history, physical geography or early V.I.P's. Although a fascinating business, etymology can be hazardous. Many people show

3

a weakness for romantic and extravagant derivations which sometimes confuse more than illuminate research into pre-industrial settlement. A usually reliable source, Ekwall's *The place names of Lancashire,* gives that it derives from an old word 'withen' meaning willow. So Withington could mean a settlement on a wet marshy area covered with willows. Another explanation is that the name comes from that of Widdingas, a Saxon chieftain who may once have lived in the area.

Until the spread of urban settlement which accompanied the industrial revolution, Withington was an area of small farms and hamlets with the occasional substantial house or hall making a contrast with the dwelling places of the poorer tenant farmers. Some of these farms can be identified on the 1911 map — Old Hall Farm (the site of the original Manor House), Old Doghouse Farm, Oaks Farm, Pinfold Farm, Hough Farm and Yew Tree Farm. The 1871 Census showed that Samuel Higginbottom, his wife Mary, their five children and one general servant lived at Yew Tree Farm. This farm occupied 52 acres on Old Hall Lane (now Old Moat Lane), and as with much of Withington, the land was owned by the Egertons. However, the establishment of the housing estates in both the nineteenth and twentieth centuries transformed this rural Withington, and those country lanes — Old Hall Lane, Raspberry Lane, Burton Lane . . . became busy roads.

Manchester people were moving out of central Manchester as it became congested and industrial, and as builders rushed to meet the demand for housing in places such as Rusholme and Withington. Strict comparison of population size at various times is not possible as boundaries have changed, but as the area of Withington was much larger in 1801 than it is today, it is undeniable that a massive growth of population has been a feature of Withington over the last 150 years. In 1801 the Census gave the population of Withington as 743, in 1901 it was 30,022, and in 1951 it was 67,718. Today Withington has a population of approximately 27,000 people, reflecting boundary changes and a fall in the average number of persons per household.

It is interesting to see the changes in the occupations of these people. The 1871 Census showed that the area corresponding to Withington today had 52 people engaged in the cotton trade, a turnpike keeper, a lamplighter, 603 live-in servants, 16 farmers, and 55 farm servants. By 1971 virtually none of these occupations would feature in the Census.

Improvements in transport between Withington and other parts of the city were necessary to meet the needs of people who were moving into Withington, and these improvements in their turn made the area more accessible and desirable. The Manchester to Wilmslow Turnpike Trust, founded in 1752, maintained and administered two of the major roads in the area, using the tollbar system, until the Trust ceased to operate in 1881. One of the Turnpike Trust's roads was Palatine Road. This road, together with the girder bridge, was opened in 1862. The Trustees purchased land for the road from landowners in the area and a tollgate was erected at the Barlow Moor Lane corner. The landowners actually sold the land at a loss, but as the opening of the road dramatically increased the value of the surrounding land, it was a shrewd move.

Rail, tram and bus transport expanded in the nineteenth century. Withington's railway station at West Didsbury opened in 1880, and horse trams commenced a service along Palatine Road and Wilmslow Road to town in c.1880. Electric trams replaced the horse trams in 1902, although horse buses and cabs remained in use for some time — there were cab stands at Mauldeth Road, the White Lion, and the terminus at West Didsbury.

Schools and churches were built to meet the educational and religious needs of the rapidly growing village. Some are still with us today, although often altered, or with a new function as the Methodist Church on Burton Road which now houses the Withington Community Association.

Withington, c.1904

Withington Police Station (on the site of the present Fire Station at the corner of Wilmslow Road and Arnfield Road), c.1910. The milestone at the pavement edge can still be seen there.

The Methodist Church on Wilmslow Road opened in 1865, the Presbyterians opened their church in Wilmslow Road in Fallowfield in 1869, the Roman Catholics opened St. Cuthbert's in 1881 (original dedication to 'The Holy Ghost and St. Cuthbert'), the Congregational Church followed in 1883; Churches not only provided religious leadership for the village, they frequently pioneered education, and acted as the main social centres (although the publicans may have disputed this). They were also able to enforce what they saw as proper behaviour on the inhabitants, as the following anecdote from The New Parochial Schools' Bazaar Handbook illustrates. 'A resolution passed at the Easter Vestry Meeting, April 12th 1855, recorded: That the Churchwardens, Sidesmen and Constable leave the Church after the First Lesson and proceed through the Parish to see that there is no disorderly conduct during the hours of divine service in conformity with the custom of other parties.' And this was no empty threat. Two men who were discovered gathering nettles to make nettle beer at a time when they should have been in church were 'taken into custody' (the words used in the pamphlet!) and held until the service was over.

Schools established in this period were St. Paul's Parochial School in 1844; a grammar school in Lansdowne Street in 1883, Carshalton High School in Heaton Road (opened during the 1880's); and a Roman Catholic school next to the church in Palatine Road in 1891.

This growth in Withington's population, first along the main roads and then on the side areas, as land belonging to the Egerton family was developed, made demands on housing, transport, health services, education, and the supply of gas and water. It must have become obvious how inadequate village administration was when faced with the complexities of city life. Withington's Local Board of Health was set up in 1876 under the Public Health Act of 1872. The offices were in Withington Town Hall in Lapwing Lane which was built in 1881 to house the Board's administration — the letters W.L.B. can still be seen today over the door. The Court Leet just faded away.

Local Boards were abolished by the Local Government Act of 1894, and were replaced by Urban District Councils. Street grids marked "Withington Local Board" — there are several in Warburton Street — serve as a reminder of the Withington Local Board's period of administration. The wards that had existed under the local board system — Withington, Fallowfield, Whalley Range, Chorlton-cum-Hardy, Didsbury and West Didsbury — remained virtually the same under the Withington U.D.C., and three councillors were elected for the Withington Ward — Mr Coombs, Mr J Bradshaw and Mr W E Howard. Margaret Ashton who was well known for her services to health and education, was elected as a member of Withington Urban District Council in 1900, and in 1908 she became the first woman to sit on the Manchester City Council.

However, just as the Court Leet, Poor Law Administration and the Local Board of Health were replaced with new developments in local government to meet the changing needs of the residents, the Withington U.D.C. also became a thing of the past. Around the turn of the century, support built up in a number of areas of Manchester for amalgamation with the city of Manchester in order to take advantage of centralised and more efficient administration of services such as transport, water supply and sewage disposal. On the 26th January, 1904, the ratepayers of Withington decided; 4086 were in favour of Withington being included in the city boundaries, 805 against, and 48 were in favour subject to the condition that a secondary school was established in the area. The six wards of the old U.D.C. became three wards of the city — Withington, Didsbury and Chorlton-cum-Hardy, each with three councillors and one alderman.

Withington's development continued under the new form of local government; the swimming baths were opened in 1911, the present library in 1927, and an extensive council housing estate was established in the Old Moat area in the inter-war years. Industry was never significant in Withington, and this feature did not alter in the twentieth century. Booker in 'A History of the Ancient Chapels of Didsbury', written in 1857, noted that Withington "had no mill or manufacture of any description, no colliery, railway, river or canal", and apart from the coming (and subsequent going) of the railway this is still largely the situation today.

The two hospitals — Christie and Withington — have been the major source of employment in the area. Withington people endured the war years, and although the bomb damage must have been catastrophic for those directly affected, the area on the whole was not badly affected. There are sometimes advantages in not having industry and docks on your doorstep.

Today Withington is a well-established, largely residential suburb and in terms of home and car ownership and levels of employment is one of Manchester's more fortunate suburbs. In this it has many similarities with Didsbury, and its history is inextricably linked with that suburb.

Didsbury Priory Lodges, Wilmslow Road (between Fog Lane and what is now Anerley Road), c.1900.

Didsbury

The name Didsbury is said to have been derived from a Saxon family name, and if so it is a guide to the antiquity of the village. It is the possible derivation of the name which has given rise to the suggestion that the chapel of mediaeval times might have been preceded by a Saxon chapel, probably built of wood.

Although Didsbury has a tenuous link with Roman times from the discovery of a coin of Antoninus Pius near Millgate Lane, not far from the ford, it is not until the 13th century that there is documentary evidence. Hollingworth, the 17th century historian, repeats the story that the chapel was built before 1235. In 1325, when there is the first mention of a cemetery, the chapel was said to be 'of antiquity beyond memory'. And in 1352, at the time of a visitation of the Great Plague or Black Death, the Lichfield Diocesan authorities again authorised the consecration of a cemetery 'in consequence of the devotion of the people of Didsbury during the late pestilence, and the

difficulty of carrying dead to Manchester'. They also authorised the celebration of divine worship in the chapel 'which though it is of antiquity beyond memory has been seldom used of late'.

The Chapelry comprised the Townships of Didsbury, Withington, Burnage, and part of Heaton Norris. The boundary between the manors of Withington and Heaton Norris divide the chapelry into two halves, with part of Burnage and part of Heaton Norris lying within the manor of Heaton Norris; and Didsbury, Withington, and part of Burnage in the manor of Withington. In those very early days agriculture was probably in its infancy here, starting in the south of the village on the well-drained soil overlying gravel, and spreading northwards as land was cleared, until by late mediaeval times only the moor and remaining woodland on the border where Withington, Didsbury, Burnage, and Heaton Norris met, was uncultivated. This area of common land in early times was not included in any of the townships but was subsequently parcelled out between the neighbouring

townships, resulting in the many rectangular strips seen on 19th century maps. Two groups of these 'detached' areas were later to be known as Barcicroft and Cotton Fields. Those detached areas of the townships were probably cultivated on the mediaeval strip system, and there is evidence from the names of fields that much, if not all, of the agricultural land of Didsbury was so farmed. The use of the word 'dole' for part of a field, and the terms 'meanfield' and 'townfield' are thought to relate to fields cultivated on the strip system, and there were many fields so named in the Didsbury township.

In the latter half of the 18th century strip farming disappeared as the Enclosure Acts came into force, and Didsbury would be no exception. By the time of the Tithe map of 1845 there were at least 48 farms in the township, and those farms changed little during the 19th century until they were overtaken by the spread of suburbia in the 40 years from about 1890 to 1930. Of those farms probably only the Stenner Lane farmhouse and the School Lane farmhouse in the car park of the former Capitol cinema have survived. Tithes were redeemed in the 19th century, but they had had a long history. When the monasteries were suppressed the tithes previously collected by the Abbots were claimed by the churches. The Warden of Manchester Collegiate Church (the present Cathedral) claimed tithes of wool, lambs, calves, hay, hemp, flax, corn, and grain. In Didsbury the claim was opposed and brought to a law-suit in the Duchy Court, presumably without success as the collection of tithes continued.

As in most post-Industrial Revolution villages, the story of Didsbury's population is one of continuous growth. During the first 60 years of the 19th century the population increased by 1210 (from 619 to 1829); it increased by a further 1200 in the next decade, and by 1500 in the decade 1871–1881, to reach 4601. And in the following 20 years it more than doubled to a figure of 9234, at which point Didsbury was absorbed into Manchester.

The availability of public transport, as of educational and religious facilities has obviously been influenced by the movement of population. Local roads were probably adequate before the 18th century for travellers on foot and horseback with little maintenance, but when wheeled vehicles began to move both goods and passengers in ever-increasing numbers, the main roads tended to become either dustbowls or quagmires, depending on the weather. As far as the trunk roads were concerned turnpiking was the answer, and it came to Didsbury with an Act of 1749 authorising turnpiking of Wilmslow Road from Ardwick Green via Fallowfield to Didsbury, and

an Act of 1752 dealing similarly with the road from Didsbury to Wilmslow. Tolls were collected at bars both on the road itself and on side roads. The side road bars at Fog Lane and Parrs Wood Lane had long lives, whilst the one at Barlow Moor Road is said to have been in place for only two years. The Trust expired in 1881, the year after the railway came to Didsbury. The railway was able to cope with the movement of both passengers and goods in quantity, and for perhaps 50 years — until the establishment of reliable petrol-driven vehicles — the railway was king. However, it lacked the flexibility and lower overheads of the new forms of road transport, and — apart from a short period

when the west coast main line was being electrified — the service became progressively poorer, until in 1967 the station closed. In the light of current developments in light rapid transit, and the probability that Didsbury will once again be served by rail, it is unfortunate that the station buildings were allowed to deteriorate to the point where there was no alternative to demolition.

In the early 19th century Didsbury already had a horse bus service to Cheadle and Manchester, and during the mid 19th century these services increased. In 1880 the Manchester Carriage Company Ltd started running horse trams as far as Withington, and later to West Didsbury, but because of opposition from influential local worthies, lines were never laid into Didsbury village. Electric trams commenced running in December 1902 between West Didsbury and Victoria Street, and between West Didsbury and Exchange, eventually becoming routes 41 and 42, whilst the Southern Cemetery circular (45 and 46) commenced in June 1913. All four services were converted to motor bus operation in February 1939.

Education in Didsbury can be traced back to the mid 17th century, when James Turner was the schoolmaster, and Didsbury chapel was possibly in use as a schoolroom. It is likely that there was a purpose-built schoolhouse as early as 1728 (a deed of 1827 refers to an ancient schoolhouse in Didsbury). This may have been the school on a site beyond the east end of Warburton Street. It was replaced in 1831 by a new school on the same site, but in 1878 the land on which it stood was bought by the Midland Railway Company for construction of the cutting which was to contain the line. The money paid by the railway company was used to build the Elm Grove Schools which may still be seen today.

Another early school was the Didsbury Village School established by the Rector of the Parish Church when he found himself unable to support his fellow trustees of the National School at Warburton Street.

Coronation Festivities, Stenner Lane Fields, 1911.

In 1861 the Methodists, whose children had previously attended the National School, felt compelled to consider building their own School, following differences with the rector of the Parish Church, and in 1863 the new school in Whitechapel Street was opened.

Twentieth century schools in Didsbury are those in Beaver Road (1909), St Catherine's (1929/1937), Didsbury Central (1930), (later Didsbury Technical High, but subsequently pulled down and replaced by St Mark's R.C. High), and Broad Oak (1955).

Wesleyan Theological Institution, c.1905

This view is of the access road at the rear of the Chapel in the grounds of the Wesleyan Theological Institution (now the Community Studies and Education site of Manchester Polytechnic). The access road and the buildings are still there but the area where the two porches can be seen is now glazed in, and is the 'Union Shop & Bar'. The hedge and trees on the left have gone, much of the site being occupied by the Simon Building; and at the far end of the road, on the left, part of the house which is now the Teachers' Resource Centre (801 Wilmslow Road) can just be seen between the hedge and the lower tree branches.

Of the churches, only the parish church (St James) and its predecessor Didsbury Chapel, have any claim to antiquity. The chapel has been mentioned earlier. It is said to have been completely rebuilt in stone in 1620 (stones in the north side of the tower tend to confirm this) and has subsequently been much altered and extended. Major rebuilding took place in 1842, and a thorough restoration was undertaken in 1855. The strange parapet of semi-circular arches on the tower date from 1801; the stones from the earlier battlements now adorn the vestry on the south side of the church.

As the centre of population began to move towards Barlow Moor Road in the mid 19th century, a need developed for a church in that part of the village, and in 1858 Emmanuel was built. Increasing population was probably the reason why the church was extended some time after 1872. St Paul's Methodist Church dates from 1877.

Ivy Cottage Church stems from the Bible class started in 1893 by Mr Oliver Brockbank in School Lane (then Hardman Street). In 1898 the class moved to 'Ivy Cottage', 18 Barlow Moor Road, in the grounds of which Mr Brockbank built a Hall, which in turn became too small to cope with the demand. He then built the present Church on the opposite side of the road. Beaver Park Baptist Church was built in 1901.

St Catherine's R.C. Church is a recent addition to the churches of Didsbury, dating from 1957. Previously Mass had been celebrated in a hall on School Lane.

Didsbury's local administration was in its own hands for a comparatively short period. From about 1662 to 1750 it was part of the Township of Withington, and prior to 1662, part of the Parish of Manchester. Between 1750 and 1876 it was a township in its own right though never with its own administrative offices. As a township it had parish constables, overseers of the poor (with its own workhouse in Grove Lane), church wardens (who also had lay duties to perform) and way wardens, who supervised and instructed the workers who maintained the roads. Probably all of these officers were unpaid.

Didsbury has never had a significant industrial presence. In the early 19th century Didsbury Mill was probably the biggest single employer of labour; then, something like a hundred years ago, Agnes Ann Heald began the expansion of a simple farming operation, culminating in the present day semi-industrial plant, which processes and distributes milk and fruit products nationwide.

Johnson's map of 1820 (left)

At this date both Withington and Didsbury were completely rural. There was little sign of movement out of Manchester by wealthy merchants and manufacturers; the effects of the Industrial Revolution were not yet beginning to be felt so far out of Manchester. In Didsbury the soft-edged shading marks the limit of land which was liable to be flooded when the Mersey burst its banks after heavy rainfall. On today's maps the river does not exactly follow the old boundary between Didsbury and Northenden, an indication that the river has changed its course since boundaries were decided in historic times.

Only Parrs Wood Hall (Parrs Wood House), Didsbury House (part of the Manchester Polytechnic Community Resources and Education site), Catholic (Catterick) Hall, Parkfield, and Withington Lodge appear as houses of any size, and all had probably been built within the preceding 30 years. Parrs Wood House is still to be seen, Didsbury House was cased in stone when the Wesleyans acquired the house, but the others have been demolished. Withington Lodge was later renamed Groombridge House, and was demolished so that the Christie Hospital could be built.

Wilmslow Road can be seen as an un-named grey tinted thread running through the map. The winding nature of this road and of Fog Lane is probably an indication of their antiquity. 'Hall' is an old Lancashire style for farm house, and three examples can be seen — Old Hall (Withington), Cabbage Hall (Fallowfield), and Lapwing Hall (West Didsbury).

Didsbury & Withington in 1910 (overleaf)

Almost 100 years after the Johnson map, which showed the two villages as being completely rural, much of the area had been built up, partly by terraced houses (Withington village, Didsbury village, and Burton Road/Cavendish Road), and partly by large semis and even larger mansions (West Didsbury). Many of the mansions remain, especially in the Fielden Park area, but others, on isolated sites, have been demolished, and the sites redeveloped. Catterick Hall, Adria House, and Didsbury Priory are examples in Fog Lane, whilst Ballbrook, Moorfield, The Hollies, and Withington House are examples on the Didsbury/Withington border. Groombridge House (Wilmslow Road/Cotton Lane) was demolished to allow the building of the first phase of Christie Hospital. In 1879, the Midland Railway had cut a swathe through the north of Didsbury, although by putting it into a cutting its effect on the village was reduced. The new line to Styal, on the other hand, was built on an embankment to allow it to cross the Mersey, the Midland line, and many roads before reaching Slade Lane Junction, where the main line was also on an embankment. Farmland was still in evidence in 1910, but almost all of it was used by Manchester Corporation in the 1920's and 30's to build Council estates.

Withington & West Didsbury Station, c.1950.

West Didsbury

West Didsbury is the area west of Palatine Road, bordered by Cavendish Road and Lapwing Lane, and by the River Mersey.

It began as a small village settlement centred on Nell Lane, connected to Withington by Burton Road, and grew through the 19th century. Although not a major suburb in the sense that Didsbury and Withington are, it does have a separate identity. This is partly a hangover from the divisions of the old Withington Board of Health, and partly due to the housing developments which took place in this area in the 1860's. The main estate, which was established by the Rusholme and Withington Estate Benefit Building Society, was named Albert Park.

As in Withington and Didsbury, when the population increased, so there was a demand for new schools and churches. Christ Church was built in 1882, Christ Church National School, Burton Road in 1890 (closing again early this century), and Cavendish Road Schools in 1904. For some time after 1945 the Lancasterian Special School was in Barlow Moor Road.

Grosvenor St Aidan's United Reformed Church in Palatine Road is an example of the church following its congregation, as it moved from All Saints, Longsight, and Withington. The 'Grosvenor' in the title relates to the early Presbyterian Church on Grosvenor Square (as it was then called), All Saints. That congregation moved to the Withington Church, as did that of Longsight, until in 1971 the combined congregation moved to St Aidan's.

Another example of a moving population is that of the Jews in South Manchester. The Withington congregation of Spanish and Portuguese Jews already had a synagogue converted from a house in Mauldeth Road (now an Adult Education Centre of the City Council), but as the population increased and moved southwards along Palatine Road, there was a demand for a more conveniently situated synagogue. The Withington congregation then built a new synagogue on Queen's (Queenston) Road, and moved to it from the Mauldeth Road building in 1926. Two years earlier, Jews descended from Arabic-speaking Sephardim, had built the Sha'are Sedek Synagogue nearby in Old Lansdowne Road.

Withington Board of Health was divided into six Wards — Withington, Fallowfield, Whalley Range, Chorlton-cum-Hardy, Didsbury, and West Didsbury. The name West Didsbury had not been accepted by everyone; there was strong support for Albert Park, and the controversy was eventually resolved by an appeal to the County Council. Fletcher Moss, in his 'Fifty Years Public Work in Didsbury', takes a sideswipe at the pretensions of the new residents in this area: 'genteel villas were springing up, as mushrooms, toadstools, or Jonah's gourd flourish in a night, and the builders knew that a name savouring of royalty would bring higher rents, so they named it Albert Park'.

The Amalgamation League, which was established to promote the incorporation of Didsbury and Withington into Manchester, started in West Didsbury. The General Committee held its first meeting in a house in Leopold Avenue in 1902, and the first public meeting was held in West Didsbury Public Hall, Burton Road. The League initially faced apathy and opposition, and a number of leading figures — Mr G H Gaddum, Mr James Heald, and Lord Egerton of Tatton — found various reasons not to be associated with the movement. However, the League eventually persuaded residents to vote for incorporation, or perhaps the residents saw for themselves the advantages of an improvement in local services, and amalgamation was achieved in 1904.

Wilmslow Road (Derby Road to White Lion)

Church closed, that congregation also joined Withington.

C A Lejeune, The Observer's film critic for so many years, was born, and lived as a child, in the house beyond the Church, Professor Hickson in the one at the left-hand of the picture. All three are now demolsihed.

Princess Christian College, Wilmslow Road, 1913

For as long as many of us can remember, the Princess Christian College has been located in a large house at the corner of Wilbraham Road and Hart Road, Fallowfield, but here is evidence that it was previously at 411–413 in these two Victorian semis next to the Arosa Hotel. (Before that the College was in Kersal.) The houses are still recognisable although the decorative stonework above the ground floor bay windows has gone, as have the garden gates. The photograph is from a postcard sent by 'A S' from 'P C College' in which she says she has 'quite settled down and likes the work, although it is hard'.

Presbyterian Church, c.1935 (above)

This church was built in 1869, at the corner of Wilmslow Road and Victoria Road, and was so situated that it would serve the Presbyterians of both Withington and Fallowfield. An example of practical Christianity was displayed by the congregation in 1875 when a house at 5 Marriott Street was taken over to set up an orphanage. The establishment, known as the Withington Orphanage, grew and moved first to 21 Burton Road, and later to larger premises which today form part of Oak Lodge Hotel.

In the 1880's there were moves to establish a further Presbyterian congregation in the Didsbury area. Between 1886 and 1889 afternoon services were held in Withington Town Hall. In 1889 it was decided to build a church, and a site was found in 1890 at the junction of Parkfield Road and Palatine Road, although the new church — St Aidan's — was not completed until 1901.

In 1940 the congregation of Grosvenor Square Church, All Saints, united with the Withington Church — to be known as Grosvenor Withington Presbyterian Church; and in 1961, when the Longsight Presbyterian

Old Post Office and Library, Wilmslow Road, 1925 (right)

The Withington Library we see today was opened in 1927, but there had been an earlier Library in a house — number 46 — on this site since 1911. This photograph shows it at the right of the picture with demolition about to commence. The middle house, here seen with its roof slates removed, was Withington Post Office, which moved from here to number 50A (formerly Hewitt's newsagents) on demolition of this house. Number 50 — the house without a roof — was the home of the two Dr Stephens, whilst in the background is 156 Wellington Road. Withington has had other libraries in the past; the photograph on page 13 shows that Hewitt's the newsagent operated a circulating library; and Withington Public Hall in Burton Road, which opened in 1861, had a library of over 1,200 books. Fletcher Moss in his book 'Fifty Years of Public Work in Didsbury' mentions the Public Hall Library: 'In 1895 and several succeeding years I moved a resolution for the adoption of the Public Libraries Act and was always sat upon by the Conservative majority. Mr Joe Lunn (Conservative,

builder) of Withington told us there was a library in Withington in an upper room somewhere behind the White Lion, and all the folk that ever went into it were a few women a week. What was the good of having another library?'

Hewitt's, Wilmslow Road, 1908 (below)

Mr W Hewitt, stationer and bookseller did business at what was then 50a Wilmslow Road from 1901 to 1916. Newspaper posters are always interesting in the way they give a quick view of the preoccupations of the day, and they can also be very useful in dating a photograph. Mr R D Darbishire, a well-known Manchester man, and after whom the Darbishire Health Centre in Rusholme is named, died on the 8th of November, 1908.

Ernest Rutherford, the physicist who lived at 17 — now 409 — Wilmslow Road between 1907 and 1919, was a regular customer at Hewitt's. The shop is now numbered 412 Wilmslow Road, and is still a newsagents.

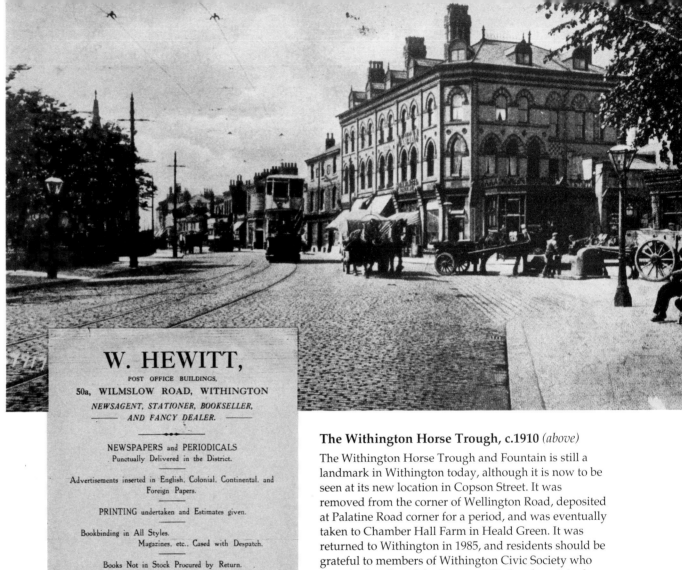

The Withington Horse Trough, c.1910 (above)

The Withington Horse Trough and Fountain is still a landmark in Withington today, although it is now to be seen at its new location in Copson Street. It was removed from the corner of Wellington Road, deposited at Palatine Road corner for a period, and was eventually taken to Chamber Hall Farm in Heald Green. It was returned to Withington in 1985, and residents should be grateful to members of Withington Civic Society who organised and paid for its return. Today the original function of providing water for working horses in the area has long passed, but the Trough serves as a pleasant reminder of pre-car Withington.

(left)

This advertising sheet hints at Edwardian times — 'colonial' is a term redolent of the days before the sun set on the Empire, and picture postcards and penny libraries are also things of the past.

Waller's Wall, Davenport Avenue, 1908 *(left)*

In 1890, the terraced houses numbered 2–24 and 13–25 Davenport Avenue were owned by Ralph Davenport Waller. Those are the houses beyond the wall in this picture. The houses on this side of the wall were owned by Hough Fullerton, and the conclusion to be drawn from the building of the wall (with spiked top) is either that Waller wished to preserve the quietness of a cul-de-sac for his tenants, or — more likely — that Fullerton was not prepared to pay towards the cost of constructing Waller's section of the road which Fullerton's tenants would need to use to have easy access to Wilmslow Road, which can be seen through the haze.

Bomb Damage at the Scala Cinema, 1940

Repairs being undertaken to the cinema and the road in front, after a hit by a small bomb on 1st October, 1940, the same night on which nine people were killed in a shelter in Withington. The Scala survived both the war and the decline in cinema audiences during the 1960's. It opened just before World War I at a time when Manchester was experiencing a boom in 'picture palaces'. By the mid 1930's, there were 109 in Manchester. Many people visited the cinema three or four times a week, and teachers complained that their pupils were neglecting their homework and were too tired to concentrate in class because of excessive cinema-going. By 1965 however, the boom was over, only 40 cinemas remaining. Before the 'talkies' caught on, many cinemas had resident pianists or organists who would play music they considered appropriate to the action taking place on the screen. The Scala's woman pianist was considered particularly good.

The films advertised here were Joan Bennett in 'The Housekeeper's Daughter' (Monday to Wednesday), and Ginger Rogers in 'Fifth Avenue Girl' (Thursday to Saturday), and a 'Matinee Today at 2.0' is promised. But this was just wartime bravado. Manchester Evening News files show that advertising ceased and did not recommence until Tuesday 22nd October when, presumably, repairs had been completed.

White Lion Hotel, Wilmslow Road, c.1870 *(below)*

There are two views of the White Lion, the old and the new. The old White Lion was originally an 18th century bulding, probably altered or rebuilt about 1840 to appear as in this picture, and replaced by the present building in 1881. The Scala (Cine City) now stands on much of the land here occupied by the White Lion. It is believed that during the early years of the 19th century, the Rush Cart was made up for its annual August procession to the Parish Church in Didsbury on Mee's Farm which stood just behind this hotel.

Burton Road (formerly Burton Lane) was originally known as White Lion Lane, presumably because it led to the White Lion. The photograph shows one of the old open-topped horse-drawn buses of the Manchester Carriage Company Ltd. with Copson Street behind.

Hibbert's, 73 Wilmslow Road, 1890's *(above)*

James Hibbert is the man with the bicycle; his wife Hannah stands in the doorway. As well as timepieces and jewellery, Hibbert also sold, according to a church pamphlet published in 1896, 'Bangles and Brooches, Spoons and Spectacles, Toothpicks and Tea-pots'. At the left of the picture is the tiled shop front of Charles Hope's butcher's shop, and in the window of Hibbert's is the reflection of the pub (The Albert) at the corner of Barbican Street.

By 1910 the shop had become part of John Williams, the grocers, and now only the upstairs windows and brickwork are recognisable, the ground floor having been much altered, and occupied by Don Camillo's at the time of writing (1988).

Old Wesleyan Chapel, Old Moat Lane, 1933
(below)

Built in 1832, this chapel situated opposite Duffy's shop was architecturally very similar to the Wesleyan chapels built in Rusholme and Levenshulme around this time — on a modest scale, with no gardens or pretensions, and just a small graveyard. Before this chapel was built, the Methodists had met in a number of rented rooms. In 1801 services were held in a house belonging to Mr Cash, a handloom weaver, which was on the site of the present Royal Bank of Scotland. In 1817 they moved to a harness room belonging to Mr Davenport, and later to another harness room owned by Mr Rylance of Burton Road. After such accommodation a chapel, however modest, must have given much satisfaction. It soon proved too small for the growing congregation and in 1865, the present Methodist Church in Wilmslow Road was opened. The old Chapel was converted into 8 back-to-back dwelling houses as seen here, and four cottages were built in the grounds. Three of these cottages — now known as Chapel Terrace — can still be seen today. They are largely unaltered, and, with their old-style windows and pretty gardens, are a charming reminder of old Withington.

    The Chapel was demolished in 1939, the site now being occupied by post-war houses. The house to the right of the Chapel has also been demolished, but beyond it can be seen numbers 43–53 Old Moat Lane which are still there today. As in other areas of Manchester, the Methodists were involved in education. In 1829 they began the first Day School and the first Sunday School in Withington.

Old Moat Lane School, May 1941 *(right)*

The school is now the Lower School of Whalley Range High School. On 7th May 1942 it was the victim of a German bombing raid when considerable damage was done to this section of the internal quad. The damaged part was subsequently rebuilt, the upper corridor enclosed, and later the ground floor corridor was also enclosed.

Old Hall Cottages, c.1890 *(below)*

The Old Hall Lane connected Withington village with Old Hall Farm, the site of which is now occupied by houses on Eddisbury Avenue. Today's Old Moat Lane follows the line of Old Hall Lane until it reaches this point, which is close to the corner of Doncaster Avenue and Old Moat Lane. The road continued to Old Hall Farm, and on the left there was a field footpath which ran across fields and the Red Lion Brook to Pinfold Farm, near the corner of what is now Abberton Road and Meltham Avenue. The cottages seen here would have been demolished shortly before the Old Moat Estate was built.

The Old Farm, Mauldeth Road and Princess Road, c.1922 *(left)*

Old Hall Farm, also known as Chorlton's Farm, has interesting links with old Withington. It replaced the original manor house, an old black and white building, in 1750. A new manor house had been built in 1596 for the then Lord of the Manor Sir Nicholas Mosley; that building, known as Hough End Hall can still be seen today near the corner of Nell Lane and Mauldeth Road.

Old Hall Farm was demolished around 1922 by the Corporation to make way for council housing. We have two reminders of that old manor house; Old Moat Lane takes its name from the moat that surrounded the manor house, and a bronze plaque on a wall in Eddisbury Avenue says 'This tablet recalls the completion of 10,000 houses built by the Corporation of Manchester to house the working-classes of the City between the years 1919 to 1928. The group of houses to which this tablet is attached stands upon the land originally enclosed by the moat of the ancient manor house of Withington, the arms of the four Lords of the Manor who held their lands in succession under the barony of Manchester being reproduced on this tablet. Unveiled September 6th 1928'.

The houses at the right-hand edge of the picture are in Mouldsworth Avenue, those without roofs being in Pownall Avenue. The newly built Princess Road crosses Old Hall Lane in the foreground, and the line of Mauldeth Road can be seen to the left of the farm buildings. Beyond that is the darker line of the Chorlton/Gorton railway, crossed by Yew Tree Road bridge. Fallowfield and Withington villages are in the distance.

Somerford Avenue, 1937

Somerford Avenue celebrates the coronation of George VI. Withington, as shown by the programme on this page, also made some effort to mark the coronation of George V on the 22nd June, 1911. Withington residents still organise events to celebrate such occasions, and the festivities arranged for the Silver Jubilee of 1977 generated such a fund of community spirit that a festival has been held each year since then.

17

The Old Forge, Burton Road, c.1880 *(above)*

A forge or smithy in Burton Road was established in 1800 and was certainly at 3 Burton Road (opposite the Public Hall, which adjoins The White Lion) in 1881 when the then owner Mr William Priday moved to new premises in Wilmslow Road (between St Paul's and the Fire Station) which can still be seen today. The business seems to have expanded with the move; Mr Priday now advertised himself as 'Coach builder, Wheelwright and Smith', as shown on the letterhead. However, the Old Forge continued as a smithy, and the 1913 directory shows William J Priday there as a blacksmith. This could be the William Priday shown as an 18-year old wheelwright's apprentice in the 1881 Census.

Withington Baths, Burton Road, 1926 *(above right)*

This aerial view shows how open the area was before Manchester Corporation commenced the development of council housing — a development that was to alter the face of the still largely rural Withington. The baths were opened in 1911 after incorporation with Manchester. Withington U.D.C. did not have a reputation for progressive attitudes towards the provision of facilities such as baths and libraries.

Whitchurch Road — on which the Baths now stand — had not been built. A corner of the cricket field with the boundary clearly marked is at the top left-hand corner. The vegetable or fruit garden at the top right was part of Hough Farm opposite Hope Street on Yew Tree Road.

Langford's Nursery, Burton Road, c.1910 *(right)*

This house was in front of the nursery on Burton Road, opposite Central Road, and was demolished about 1930. Jonathan Langford was a 'market gardener and nurseryman', according to the 1881 Census, employing 5 men and 1 boy, two of the men being Irish-born labourers, living in. His sons William (25) and Samuel (19) also worked in the nursery. All the family were born in Withington, Alice Langford as long ago as 1827, and at least one member of the family still lives in the vicinity.

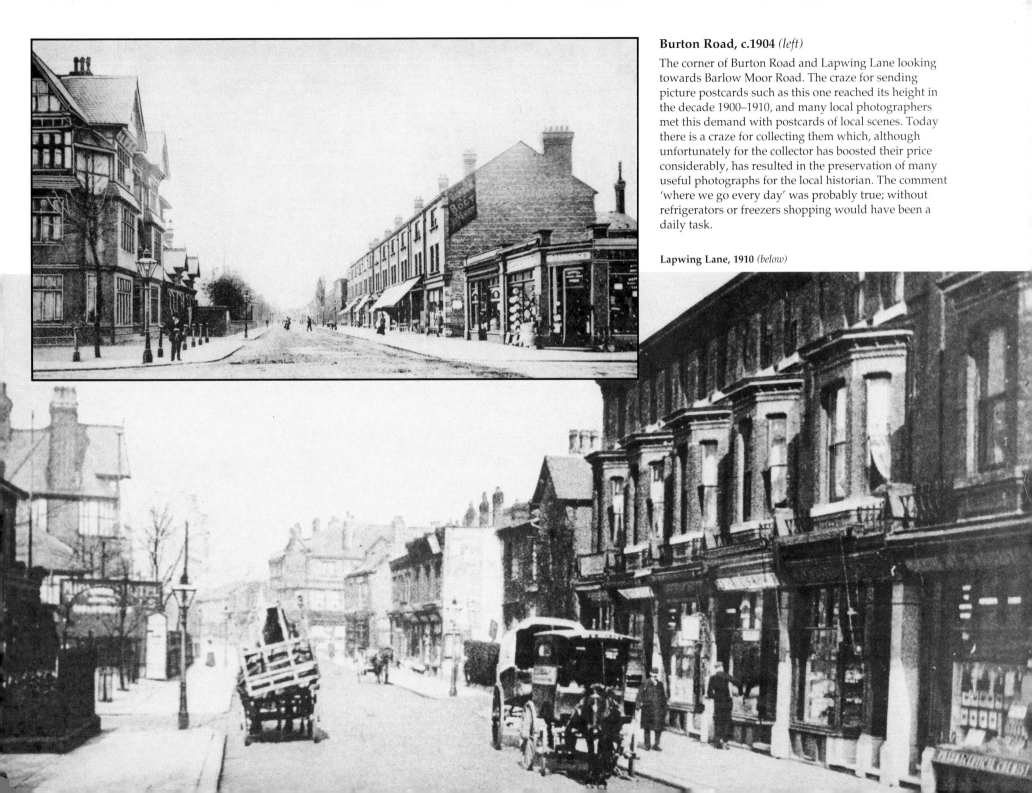

Burton Road, c.1904 *(left)*

The corner of Burton Road and Lapwing Lane looking towards Barlow Moor Road. The craze for sending picture postcards such as this one reached its height in the decade 1900–1910, and many local photographers met this demand with postcards of local scenes. Today there is a craze for collecting them which, although unfortunately for the collector has boosted their price considerably, has resulted in the preservation of many useful photographs for the local historian. The comment 'where we go every day' was probably true; without refrigerators or freezers shopping would have been a daily task.

Lapwing Lane, 1910 *(below)*

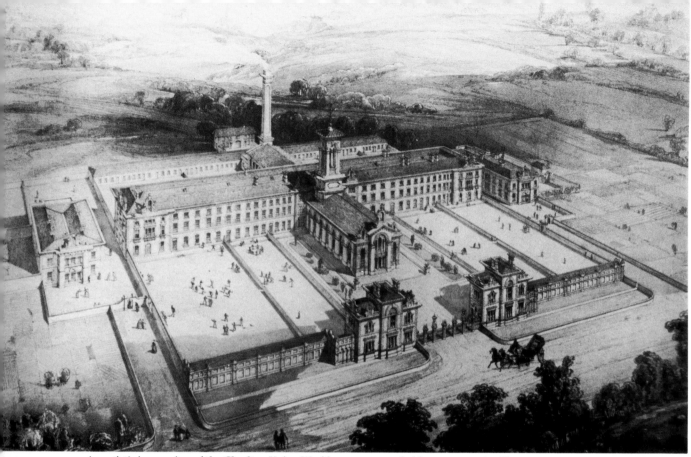

An artist's impression of the Chorlton Union Workhouse, surrounded by open countryside.

Chorlton Union Workhouse, Nell Lane *(left)*

Before the building of Chorlton Union Workhouse in 1855, the local poor were offered shelter in a few houses at the corner of Burton Road and Lapwing Lane which were known as Withington's Poor Houses. Under the Poor Law Act of 1835 Withington, Didsbury, Chorlton-on-Medlock, Ardwick, Hulme, Burnage, Stretford, Chorlton-cum-Hardy, Levenshulme, Gorton, Moss Side, Openshaw and Rusholme, were amalgamated into the Chorlton Union. Each parish was represented on the Board of Guardians which was responsible for the distribution of poor relief. Those unable to support themselves were offered food and shelter at the Workhouse, and in return, the able-bodied were expected to work at various tasks. Over the years the Chorlton Workhouse found that its role had changed from providing food and shelter to that of caring for the sick who were unable to afford medical care. Today's Withington Hospital had its origins in the old Workhouse.

New hospital pavilions to a design by Thomas Worthington (and approved by Florence Nightingale) were built across the road from the Workhouse commencing in 1864, becoming Newholme Old Peoples' Home almost 100 years later.

One man who did much to change the depressing nature of the Workhouse was Dr J Milson Rhodes (1847–1909). Dr Rhodes, who had a practice in Didsbury, was elected to the Chorlton Board in 1880. He was very concerned at the treatment the poor received, the herding together of the sick, the old, the disabled and the unemployed; the treatment of children, and the lack of proper medical care of the sick, and he made many improvements. Following his death a memorial clock and drinking fountain were erected in front of Didsbury Railway Station as a tribute. The clock is inscribed 'A Friend to Humanity'.

The quality of life enjoyed by the inmates of the Workhouse might not have been too bad compared with the prospects facing the poor who remained outside in a pre-Welfare State society. However, many did regard the possibility of ending up in the Workhouse with dread, and it is said that at one time elderly people did not like going to Withington Hospital because of its association with the old Workhouse.

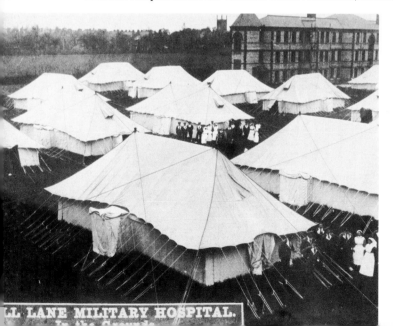

Nell Lane Military Hospital, c.1917 *(left)*

The carnage in the 1914–1918 War resulted in the use of many schools and other buildings as hospitals for wounded soldiers. Here, in a view from the corner of Tintern Avenue and Nell Lane, is part of a tented hospital, together with one of the Thomas Worthington designed 'pavilions' of the hospital department of Chorlton Union Workhouse, latterly part of Newholme Old People's Home. To the left of the pavilion is Christ Church, West Didsbury, when it still possessed its tower pinnacles, and to the left of the church can be seen houses in the Rowsley Avenue and Darley Avenue area. Most of the foreground is now occupied by Withington Hospital's visitor car park. Elizabeth Slinger Road runs through the site formerly occupied by the pavilion.

Chorlton Union Workhouse, c.1910 *(above)*

Staff of the Workhouse are here seen assembled inside the main gates of what is now Withington Hospital, with Nell Lane immediately beyond the gates, and, across Nell Lane, the main buildings of the hospital department of Chorlton Union Workhouse, which for many years before their demolition, were part of Manchester Corporation's 'Newholme' Old People's Home.

Christ Church Avenue and Barlow Moor Road, c.1920 *(above right)*

This view of Christ Church Avenue, looking south towards Wythenshawe, shows how that road looked before it was widened and extended to link the council estate at Wythenshawe with the rest of the city. It was then renamed Princess Road. All the buildings in this view have now been demolished and the junction of Princess Road and Barlow Moor Road has become much more complex.

Palatine Picture House and Cafe, c.1960 *(right)*

The end of an era. The cinema on Palatine Road closed about 1960, and the top two floors were subsequently taken down.

The Terminus, Palatine Road and Lapwing Lane, 1920's (right)

This photograph shows one of the old open-topped buses, pleasant enough for a summer trip to the seaside, but miserable travelling for much of the year. Motor buses had replaced the horse-drawn buses on the Palatine Road route in 1906.

In 1882, the Manchester Carriage and Tramways Company opened a horse tram service from Palatine Road to Central Manchester. Horse trams were replaced by electric trams from 1901 when Manchester Corporation re-organised the tram system — the new trams were quicker, cheaper and could accommodate more passengers. They commenced the run between West Didsbury and the old Exchange Station in 1902. Eventually buses replaced the trams, the last one on this route running in 1939.

Withington & West Didsbury Railway Station, c.1930 (left)

A splendidly nostalgic photograph with those old-fashioned lamps and billowing steam! The opening of the Midland Railway in 1880 contributed towards the rapid growth in Withington and Didsbury's populations. The station was originally known as Withington and Albert Park — Albert Park was the name of a housing estate built in the 1860's in the Clyde Road, Old Lansdowne Road and Cresswell Grove area, and the name did not change to West Didsbury until 1895.

Here an ex-Midland Railway 0–6–4T (one of the so-called Block Tanks) hauls a train of ex-Midland close-coupled coaches on a local train from Central Station.

Northern Lawn Tennis Club, Palatine Road, c.1913 *(above left)*

The Northern Lawn Tennis Club came to Didsbury in 1909, after having been at Old Trafford since 1882. The two-storey black and white timbered building seen here had originally been at the Old Trafford ground, but was taken down and re-erected at Palatine Road at the end of the 1909 season.

The trees are in the grounds of 119–123 Palatine Road, and the chimney stacks between the telegraph pole and marquee are those of the Bank at the corner of Palatine Road and Lapwing Lane.

The upper of the two white banners at the left of the main pavilion displays the name 'J C Parke', and it is likely that the players seen here are J C Parke and Mrs Larcombe. Parke had won the Australian singles in 1912, and was a Davis Cup player for Britain between 1908 and 1920. He and Mrs Larcombe won the mixed doubles of the Northern Tournament in 1912, 1913 and 1914. Parke was wounded at Gallipoli in 1915 but survived the War to win the first post-War singles of the Northern Tournament.

Clyde Road and Lapwing Lane, c.1885 *(above right)*

The West Didsbury area developed into a solid residential neighbourhood from the 1860's onwards, as shown by these buildings.

Withington Literary and Social Society, c.1935

The Withington Literary and Social Society was one of the many organisations set up under the umbrella of the Spanish & Portuguese Synagogue in Queen's (now Queenston) Road, West Didsbury, during the period when Rev Pereira Mendoza was minister. It was formed about 1928, shortly after the Mauldeth Road congregation moved to the newly-built Synagogue, and although — as here — it performed secular plays, this was really because only a thin repertoire of Jewish interest plays was available. The writing of such plays received much encouragement during the 1930's, and as a result many new plays were published.

The Society was active in the drama field until the war brought a temporary end to dramatics, and although it survived until about 1980, there was no longer the enthusiasm among younger members for putting on plays. It was not until 1956 that the Synagogue had its own permanent hall, and because the previous wooden building was inadequate the plays were produced at the West Didsbury Public Hall in Burton Road (now adapted for use as a supermarket).

82 Palatine Road, West Didsbury, 1904 *(below)*

This former Turnpike Road was built through the fields of Withington and Didsbury in 1861, and remained turnpiked until 1881. In the distance the bend of Palatine Road where it crosses Lapwing Lane can be seen. Lapwing Farm stood at that corner until demolished to allow construction of the road. The bend at Lapwing Lane allowed Palatine Road to be aligned to follow the line of the long, narrow field known as Rushy Field, and it is this part of Palatine Road which is seen here.

The gatepost at the left of the picture belongs to Darwin House. The directory for 1891 shows Heinrich Simon as the occupier. Henry Simon was the founder of the Simon Engineering Group. France and Woodall record that the house was named after Charles Darwin. Number 82 — the nearest complete house in the picture — was the home of Edwin Butterworth a 'paper stock merchant employing 300 hands' in 1881. His 18 year old son, Edwin, was also in the business, and presumably the present day firm of Edwin Butterworth (Waste Paper) Ltd originated with this family. Next door again was at one time the home of William E Cary, the spring manufacturer, of Red Bank.

All the houses are still there today, though number 80 (now number 128) has had an extra storey added; number 82 (now number 130) is known as Martinez Luxury Apartments.

Tripps Corner — Barlow Moor Road, Palatine Road, c.1900 *(below right)*

At the turn of the century, black and white frontages were all the rage. These 'olde shoppes' were probably built on to old cottages, and would be newly opened at the time of the photograph. The boy at the right has a flag-pole over his left shoulder — probably with the Union Flag, as the poster at one of the Post Office doorways announces 'Boers Stampede Before Roberts'. At that time the Boer War generated strong nationalist feelings among the population in the face of threats to expansion of the Empire. In recent years the Post Office has occupied the left-hand shop, the off-licence the centre shop, whilst the right-hand shop has been a dress shop for many years. Much of the ornamental black strapwork on the frontage has gone, as has the Victorian gas lamp.

Toll-bar, c.1875 *(right)*

This rather splendid looking toll-house at the corner of Palatine Road and Barlow Moor Road, was operated by the Manchester to Wilmslow Turnpike Trust from 1862 to 1881. Palatine Road (known as Northenden New Road before the Post Office protested that the name would cause confusion) and the girder bridge at Northenden were opened in 1862. It must have been a boon for those travelling from this area of Withington to Altrincham as they no longer had to use the ford or the ferry at the river crossing in Northenden. The Trust managed a number of toll-bars in the locality; a photograph of one at the corner of Mauldeth Road and Wilmslow Road can be seen in *Looking Back at Rusholme and Fallowfield*. The Local Board of Health was established in 1876, and the maintenance of roads passed from the Turnpike Trust to the local authority when the Trust expired in 1881. In this picture, Hawthornden (on Palatine Road near the corner of Barlow Moor Road) can be seen at the right.

Barlow Moor Road, c.1914 (left)

Here is a traffic-free view of Barlow Moor Road, looking towards Wilmslow Road, when riding a horse along a main road was not unusual. Steam rollers continued in use on road maintenance until the 1940's when diesel-engined road rollers made their appearance. The gated road on the right is Holme Road. The wall at the corner is still there, but the silver birch just behind the wall is now in the garden of one of a group of modern detached houses, most of the high wall has gone, and the trees generally have matured, almost forming an arch over the road.

Wilmslow Road (White Lion to Fog Lane)

St Paul's School, Class II, 1922 (below left)

St Paul's Parish Church was opened in 1841 and the school in 1844. In 1896 an appeal was launched for a new school, and a pamphlet produced for a fund-raising Floral Bazaar described this early school. 'The Schools were built at a cost of £600, and opened on October 14th, 1844 with accommodation for 160 children. The site was given by Wilbraham Egerton, Esq., the principal contributors being T Carrill Worsley, Robert Gladstone, Edmund Wright and Nathan Slater, Esquires, each £50; John Souchay, Esq., £25; Bulkeley Price, D R Davies, F Hodgson, Esquires, and the Rev W F H Hooper each £20; and Government Grant £100. Prior to this school being opened a Day School was held in the Schoolroom underneath the old Wesleyan Chapel in Old Hall Lane which is now converted into cottages.'

The pamphlet also warned Withington rate-payers that if they did not financially support this new school, a School Board would be established in Withington and this would increase their rates.

It is said that one of the school's headmasters — Mr Scholes — was opposed to corporal punishment, and devised an alternative punishment whereby miscreants were involved in the hard work of pumping the bellows at the neighbouring Forge during playtime. The teacher in the photo is Mrs Jones.

Arnfield Road, Withington, October 1940 *(below)*

The German bombing raids of World War II killed over 500 people in Manchester, and thousands of houses were badly damaged. Withington, although it lacked any major military targets, suffered with the rest of the city, and ordinary people struggled to rebuild their houses and lives after the sort of destruction and devastation that is hard to imagine today.

In the most serious air raid of the War, in Withington, the Gadsby's house at 4 Arnfield Road was damaged beyond repair; the house to be seen on the site now is a replacement built in the immediate post-war period. Here policemen, with gas masks and steel helmets slung over their shoulders, guard the property. The mound in the garden is over the Anderson shelter. More than 39,000 of these shelters — named after the then Home Secretary Sir John Anderson — were dug into Manchester gardens. Fortunately, Mr and Mrs Gadsby were in the shelter when the bomb fell, and escaped injury although they were very badly shaken.

In the same raid a shelter in Burton Road was hit, killing all nine occupants; and a parachute bomb was caught up in trees close to St Paul's Church, being defused while it was still suspended in the air.

The Red Lion, Wilmslow Road, 1932 *(below)*

The Court Leet, an early form of local government, is said to have met at this pub, with the last meeting held in 1841. The Court Leet judged on matters such as stray dogs, adulterated food, wandering swine etc., and had the power to impose fines. As well as the Court Leet, the Trustees of the Turnpike Trust also used the Red Lion as a meeting place.

The present Red Lion building is over 200 years old, and there was probably an earlier public house on this site. Note the real ale in the real barrels on the back of the lorry.

In the background are the rooflights of the Electricity sub-station, which was demolished after the War, and the site redeveloped; to its right is part of the roof of St Cuthbert's R C Church.

This billhead produced for William J Priday shows The Forge in Wilmslow Road with St Paul's Church, Withington in the background. The site is being redeveloped for housing, but the front block will be retained, and the arched windows, to the left of the coach entrance, restored.

Old Cottages, Wilmslow Road, 1940 *(above)*

These cottages, known as Prospect Place, were probably farm workers' cottages before Withington was developed as a suburb of Manchester, but by 1940 all the tenants had gone, and the cottages were carefully boarded up. In 1889 the tenants were a gardener, a labourer, a cab driver, and a paviour.

The site is now occupied by a block of flats — Clifford House — which can be seen almost opposite Oak Road. Wilmslow Road was numbered in three series before about 1950: Rusholme, then Withington, and finally Didsbury. But then all main roads running through more than one of the old authorities' areas were renumbered into one sequence. These houses did not survive long enough to be renumbered.

The Toll House, Fog Lane, 1914 *(above right)*

In the 19th century, field drainage ditches bringing water from the Burnage Lane area formed two streams, one of which flowed through what is now Fog Lane, and across the cul-de-sac end of Fairfax Avenue whilst the other flowed through the grounds of Catterick Hall, Adria House and Didsbury Priory, on the south side of Fog Lane.

At a point nearly opposite Fairfax Avenue this stream crossed Fog Lane, and the picture shows the rebuilding of the culvert through which it crosses Fog Lane. The Toll House (formerly Barfield Cottage) is easily recognisable, with the grounds of Binswood on the left. The stream, which is here known as the Ball Brook, runs at the foot of the gardens of houses on the

west side of Fairfax Avenue before joining the stream from Fog Lane Park and crossing Wilmslow Road at Ballbrook Court. It there forms the old boundary between Withington and Didsbury.

Just on the border with Didsbury, Fog Lane Park is the only park in the Withington area. It covers 48 acres, and the land was acquired by the Corporation in 1926. The park was created by men employed under a scheme financed by the Ministry of Health to provide work for some of the thousands who were unemployed at this time.

A toll-bar operated at Fog Lane from 1830 to 1861, and there were also toll-bars at Burton Lane (now Road), Cotton Lane and Mauldeth Road. Toll-bars were erected on side roads to prevent people avoiding paying toll on the Manchester to Wilmslow turnpike by entering and leaving it at various points. In 1845 the charges were as follows:– a horse, 1d; a milk cart, 2d; a gig, 3d; a horse and cart, 3d; and a carriage 4½d. These takings went towards the upkeep of the roads and from them the tollgate keeper Thomas Renshaw, received a 5/– a week wage.

Fog Lane, c.1925 *(right)*

Fog Lane is seen here before the building of Parrs Wood Road which now crosses at about the place where the figure can be seen. The house on the left is 218 Fog Lane, at the corner of Ellesmere Road. The site on which the Parrs Wood Road United Reformed Church was built is the area between the nearest telegraph pole and the tree at the right of the picture.

Pytha Fold Farm (now Paulhan Rd.), 1910 *(left)*

History was made in the early hours of Thursday, April 28th 1910, when Paulhan and Grahame-White competed for a prize of £10,000 offered by the Daily Mail for the first flight from London to Manchester. They were allowed two stops en route, but Paulhan made do with only one, at Lichfield. He arrived shortly after 5.30 a.m., but even at that early hour there were crowds waiting to see the arrival.

The field was in an area known as Barcicroft in which there had been, in the 18th century, an alternation of strips of land some of which were part of Didsbury, and others part of Burnage or Withington. Possibly, in earlier times, this area and the nearby Cottonfield were heath, moorland, or woodland, and not then included within the boundaries of either Didsbury, Burnage or Withington.

Although Burnage Station had not then been completed, two special trains had been chartered, one to bring Paulhan's friends and mechanics, the other to take Paulhan and his party back to London Road Station from where they were driven to the Queens Hotel.

Grahame-White failed to complete the course due to mechanical problems.

Old Cottages, Fog Lane, c.1900 *(below left)*

At the Burnage end of Fog Lane there were two groups of old cottages. Most of them were close to the corner of Burnage Lane and Fog Lane, but this outlying group, near to what is now Burnage Station, were in Didsbury township. At the turn of the century the directories show that they were occupied by a pattern maker, a smith, a gardener, two bricksetters, and 'householders' — usually pensioners or widows. In the 19th century they were known as Cotton Shops, a name probably related to the nearby Cottonfield. They were demolished and replaced by shops about 1960.

Lapwing Lane, c.1900 *(left)*

Lapwing Lane looking from Pine Road towards Wilmslow Road at its junction with Fog Lane. The wall of Didsbury Priory apparently closes the narrow opening of Fog Lane at the far end. The south side of Lapwing Lane — behind the railings — was still open ground at this date, possibly part of what was Lapwing Hall Farm until that farmhouse was demolished in or shortly before 1862, when Palatine Road was made.

Wilmslow Road (Fog Lane to School Lane)

Didsbury Priory, c.1905 (right)

Didsbury Priory was a large house built for Mr J D Souchay, a Manchester merchant, and then called Eltville. (One of Mr Souchay's daughters was married at St Paul's Church, Withington, in the first wedding to take place there.) The house was built at the corner of Fog Lane and Wilmslow Road, on a site bounded by Clayton Avenue and Clothorn Avenue, and its name was changed from Eltville to Didsbury Priory when James Clayton Chorlton bought it in 1888. The Ball Brook was then an open stream running through the grounds behind the house, before crossing Fog Lane close to its junction with Wilmslow Road. The entrance to the grounds was in Wilmslow Road with substantial lodges on either side of the gate, in the same style as the house, with matching bargeboarding and detailing.

One picture shows the house and garden with Mr and Mrs Chorlton (both in dark clothes) and possibly their children Evelyn, Roger, Florence, and Roger's wife. Although the gardens were private, the public were allowed in when the crocuses were flowering, and many Didsbury residents made use of this concession. The second picture shows cattle being driven past the entrance and towards the Fog Lane crossing.

Parkfield Road South, c.1930 (left)

Parkfield Road South, is seen here when the trees were about 20 years old. The house on the left is Swallowhurst (number 3). Its stained glass above the porch can still be seen, but the chimney stack of the next house, beyond the private road leading to the Northern Tennis Club ground, has been taken down. The car is a Riley Mk IV Tourer of 1930 vintage.

1902 Coronation Festivities (left)

The Emblematical Car 'Army and Navy' is standing in front of 639 Wilmslow Road (corner of Clothorn Road). The 'soldier' uniforms presumably relate to those worn during the Boer War, from which the Scout uniforms of the 20th century are derived. The three people standing at the side of the car seem to be unrelated to the subject.

Didsbury War Memorial, 2nd July 1921 (below)

The scene is a Saturday evening in Wilmslow Road in front of the library on the occasion of the unveiling of the memorial to the 174 men killed in The Great War. The memorial was unveiled by Lord Derby, service prayers and lesson read by Rev W J Moulton (Principal of Didsbury College and ex-Chaplain to 62nd Division), dedicated by Rev C C Ellis (Rector of Didsbury), and handed over to the Lord Mayor by Dr Crowe (Chairman of the Committee).

Most of the buildings in this picture survive. The exceptions are the garage and adjoining cottage, replaced by two shops. Just behind the platform there appears to be a sapling tree. Today, two full grown oaks can be seen there.

Didsbury c.1860 and c.1866 (below left & right)

The earlier picture — 'A Bit of Old Didsbury' — shows the village before the arrival of the railway. Hardman Street (now School Lane) is on the right, with 'The Wellington' at the corner of Barlow Moor Road on the left. The shops at the right appear to be cottages to which have been added a Victorian shop front and upstairs room, long ago replaced by the present Pritchard's Commercial Place. The farthest terrace on the right would have been pulled down to allow the railway and station to be built in 1879, and that in its turn has gone.

In 1866 much building was taking place in Didsbury. The Wellington reflects the changing circumstances, having improved its image by adding bay windows. The painted sign on the gable end read 'Bowling Green'. The horse bus operated by the Manchester Carriage Company Ltd was about to leave, travelling via Withington and Rusholme to Market Street. Thomas Donley was licensee from 1866 to 1870; the Manchester Carriage Company Ltd was formed in 1865, and this may have been an early appearance of one of the Company's buses.

In both pictures there are signs — rather like street nameplates — on the corner below the upstairs window of The Wellington. The one on the Barlow Moor Road frontage reads 'Good Stabling', but the other has not so far been deciphered. Suspended from the corner of the building just above these signs is a strange device in two parts, the upper part apparently a pile of three logs (cigars?) and the lower a bunch of grapes(?). The authors would appreciate any help in interpreting this device.

Wilmslow Road/Hardman Street (now School Lane), 1913 (right)

This obviously-posed picture shows two Corporation horse-drawn carts of a type which was common on Manchester streets in the first 40 years of the century. The shop on the left-hand corner (now BSM Radio but then Merrill's the butchers, complete with rails for the display of fowl, rabbits, etc.) is part of the block of buildings of 1881. Beyond it the cottages have been demolished apart from the first two which have been converted into shops. At the right of the picture is the Bridgewater Collieries yard. The street is paved with the large stone setts used on side roads, in comparison with the smaller granite setts used on main roads, where traffic was heavier. Both types can still be sometimes seen when road works take place.

Wilmslow Road/School Lane corner, 1924 *(right)*

In 1924 School Lane was still known as Hardman Street, and it was probably not renamed until the terraced houses on the right were demolished and their site — and that of the colliery yard — incorporated into the widened road. The Bridgewater Collieries yard had been here since at least 1858 when it was described as 'Bridgewater Trustees Coal Wharf (Sam Sharples, agent), Barlow Moor'. The part of the site to the right of the group of men is now occupied by a single-storey estate agent's office, and, even now, if you look carefully, you will be able to make out the remains of the painted advertisement on the gable end of the shop adjoining the estate agent's. The shops at the left of the picture were built in 1881, the year after the opening of the railway.

Hardman Street (School Lane), 1924 *(left)*

On the right of this view looking towards Wilmslow Road from the railway bridge, is a coal yard, then Ogden Street continuing round to Warburton Street. On the left of the street are the terraced houses demolished to widen Hardman Street (School Lane). Advertising in those days had a much more local flavour; here the only nationally-distributed product is Bovril. Below that is a notice about a lacrosse match and on the Hardman Street frontage, a poster advertising the Scala, Withington. Another cinema, the Didsbury, in Elm Grove, is also represented, together with the Hallé — the last concert of the season was as early as March 13th — and there are two notices for Manchester auctions, as well as one for The Fellowship of Freedom and Reform, and one for a demonstration at the Houldsworth Hall on How to Dress Well.

Street lighting was still by gas of course, the farthest poles being the fluted, Lancashire County version, and the nearest, the Manchester Corporation type with its decorative base.

School Lane near Winifred Street (now Road), 1924 (below left)

School Lane looking over the hump-backed railway bridge towards Wilmslow Road. Telegraph poles are prominent carrying telephone wires to and from the exchange. Advertising is again in evidence — Little Nellie Kelly, and Rudolph Valentino as The Sheikh are on the posters.

Plans had been made in the 1930's to replace the hump-backed bridge by a girder bridge, and the girders were on the site in 1939 ready to commence work when war intervened. The girders remained there for some 30 years, but were eventually removed, and it was not until 1987 — almost 50 years later than originally planned — that the new bridge was constructed. The narrowing of the road near Winifred Street can still be seen, but scout huts now stand on part of the site of these terraced houses.

Laundry Workers, Dundonald Road, c.1911 (below)

Provincial Laundries Ltd came to Didsbury in 1911 and this photograph of the staff probably dates from about that time. The advent of the washing machine and launderette must have made life difficult for the Provincial, and it closed about 1980. The site of the laundry in Dundonald Road is now occupied by modern houses. The houses in the background of the picture may be those at the railway end of Ladysmith Road.

Provincial Laundry, 1926 (below right)

The tradition of using horse-drawn carts, or 'floats', for staging mobile tableaux survived until at least 1926 when Provincial Laundries entered this display of fashions in the Didsbury Carnival of that year. Mrs Nellie Woodhall as a child can be seen as the farthest right of the small children, and Kath Wilson is close to centre with Alice band and pigtails. Mr Brown, the Provincial Laundries vanman at the time, is in charge of the horse, with the laundry building in the background.

Sandhurst Road Bridge, 1927 *(left)*

When the Midland Railway line was built, two bridges were needed to give access to farmland which had been cut off by the railway. One was on the line of Sandhurst Road (for Whitehall Farm), and one on the old alignment of School Lane (for School Lane Farm). In the 1920's, when houses were being built on the farmland, there appeared to be plans to drive a road — Sandhurst Road — through from School Lane to Wilmslow Road, and so the access road bridge was replaced by the present, more-substantial, girder bridge. It is shown here as the first girder was being lowered into position by the railway's steam crane. Beyond the crane's jib are houses in Kingsfield Road, numbers 50 and 52 facing the crane, and 73 and 75 under construction, partly hidden by the jib.

Capitol Cinema, 1932 and 1936 *(below left & right)*

The first picture of the Capitol shows the scene in April 1932, after fire had ravaged the building. By August 1933 the cinema had been rebuilt, and three years later — in the second picture — the rebuilt cinema is tempting fate by showing 'Dante's Inferno'! Also in the second picture, one of the first Belisha beacons, named after the then Minister of Transport, Leslie Hore-Belisha, can be seen at the kerb on the corner. The beacons were the first attempts to give pedestrians legal precedence over vehicles at specified places, and were a response to the tremendous increase — as it then appeared to be — in the numbers of motor vehicles on the roads.

Wilmslow Road (School Lane to Stenner Lane)

Peacock's, Didsbury village, c.1910 *(right)*

William Peacock's business was established in 1804, possibly in these premises, and at a time when it was often the case that the village joiner was also the undertaker. This picture is thought to show Mr Bert Peacock as a young man, and it also shows the display case which contains two of the glass 'bells', protecting artificial flowers, which might have been seen on graves at that time. At the back of the case appears to be a framed certificate which would probably be Mr Peacock's professional qualification.

Ship Canal Celebrations 1885 *(right)*

Daniel Adamson, whose portrait appears above the banner, was responsible for organising support for the proposed Manchester Ship Canal. In May 1884 when the Ship Canal Bill had been passed by the Lords' Committee, Adamson was feted on his return to Didsbury. However, the Bill failed to win the support of the House of Commons, and it was not until August 8th 1885 that another Ship Canal Bill was approved by Parliament. Adamson again returned to a hero's welcome, he and his wife driving from Stockport Station to Didsbury in their landau, travelling via Fog Lane and Wilmslow Road. This is the scene which would have met them on the last leg of their journey. On the left are the shops at the corner of Old Oak Street, next to the Royal Oak pub, and then more shops up to Elm Grove. The land between there and Grange Lane was fenced at that time, possibly in preparation for the building of shops which now occupy the site. The trees beyond were in the grounds of Manor House.

The caption on the photograph suggests that this is the 1884 celebration. An unknown hand has altered the date to 1885, and certainly the wording on the Triumphal Arch was that displayed in 1885.

Coronation Festivities, 1911 *(below)*

Part of the procession of decorated floats is making its way through the village on 22nd June 1911. All the buildings seen here (except the distant railway station) survive, although shop fronts have been added to some of the old cottages. The entrance to Albert Street (now Albert Hill Street) is just beyond the chair on the pavement, and the picture was probably taken from an upstairs room of what is now Hargreaves & Company's premises. The Wellington (corner of Barlow Moor Road and Wilmslow Road) is sporting an ensign with the Union Flag in the canton and the word 'Wellington' across the lower half.

Wesleyan Sunday School Procession, c.1908 *(below)*

The procession is seen here assembling on Chapel Street (now Whitechapel Street) at the corner of Cross Street (now Crossway). The houses in the background are in Church Street. Little has changed here in the intervening years, though the gas street lighting has gone, and an extension has been built on to the school in the corner at the right of the picture. The Day School was built in 1861 at a time when Methodists' children had no choice but to attend the Church of England School. Additions were made in 1871 (fronting Crossway) and in the 1930's (at the corner of Crossway and Whitechapel). Its use as a day school finished at about the time of Didsbury's amalgamation with Manchester.

Mr William Taylor, of 22 Spring Gardens (now Springdale Gardens) just happened to be cycling past. He had been butler to Mr Thomas Ashton at Ford Bank for many years.

Wilmslow Road near Grove Lane, 1910

The shop at the left of the picture, on the corner of Grove Lane and Wilmslow Road, was a confectioner's (Miss Susie Whitehead's) separated by an entry from Charles Richardson's hairdresser's shop. Whilst the pavement is clean the same cannot be said of the roadway, which shows the effects of steel-tyred horse-drawn lorries.

The buildings seen here have completely disappeared, replaced by a block of modern shops and offices, of which Oxfam is one tenant.

Home Guard, c.1943 *(below right)*

During World War II men not in HM Forces could volunteer — or sometimes were directed — for service in the Home Guard (originally the Local Defence Volunteers), and were trained in defence techniques in case the country was invaded. This group, 'B' (Didsbury) Company, 46th Bn. County of Lancaster Home Guard was Didsbury's 'Dad's Army', and they are seen here in the schoolyard of what is now Didsbury C of E Primary School (originally Didsbury National School, built with Midland Railway Company money), Grange Lane. The buildings have since been altered by the addition of a new entrance beneath the gable, re-roofing, and removal of the ventilator on the roof ridge.

The men did not train here but in the Boys' Club building on Elm Grove; the school playground would just be a convenient place for photography. In this picture CSM Hankinson is centre front holding a shield, and immediately behind him is the CO, Captain Fred Mackenzie. The shield is probably the Rothband Trophy which the Company won in 1943 and again in 1944.

Ford Lane, 1927 (above)

The old lodge and, perhaps coachman's house, of Broomcroft. This part of Ford Lane is now a backwater of the realigned Ford Lane, and although the buildings seen here have gone, the walls on both sides of the lane remain.

Mr & Mrs Gladstone at Ford Bank, 1889

Early in December 1889, when William Ewart Gladstone had already been Prime Minister for three periods, he came to Manchester to speak to 'a vast audience' of Liberals in the Free Trade Hall. Whilst in Manchester he and his wife were guests of Thomas Ashton at Ford Bank, and they are here seen on the steps of the house. Mr Ashton died in 1898, and his son — Thomas Gair Ashton, a Liberal MP and subsequently Lord Ashton of Hyde — gave up the house. Ford Bank had previously been owned and occupied by the Birley family, but on the death of Joseph Birley's widow in 1857 or 1858, it was bought by Thomas Ashton.

In about 1899 Mrs Agnes Ann Heald bought the house, and continued to live in it for some 30 years. The directories show a change of occupation between 1925 and 1930 — presumably on Mrs Heald's death — and the 1934 directory has the last entry for Ford Bank. At about that time what had been the largest of all Didsbury's great houses was sold, and the land used for building the present estate.

Didsbury Show, 1949 (above)

The Didsbury & South Manchester Agricultural Society held a Show each year, latterly on Simon's Field, between Stenner Lane and Ford Lane. The picture shows that in 1949 it was well attended; and in 1960 there were 12,000 visitors. But when Lord Simon died and the Field became the property of Manchester Corporation, it is said that the Corporation would not allow the Society its traditional free use of the Field, and furthermore would not let it on August Bank Holiday, so that the Show of 1966 was the last of a long series.

Wilmslow Road near Sandhurst Road, 1911 *(below)*

The Sunday School's banner was first used on Whit Friday, 9th June 1911, and this may well have been the occasion. The buildings on the left are outbuildings of Lawnhurst, and the wall on the right that of Broome House.

Coronation Procession, 1911 *(below right)*

On June 22nd 1911, Didsbury celebrated the Coronation of King George V with parties for the young and old, but — in the words of Fletcher Moss — 'the great glory of the . . . festivities . . . was the procession' representing the culmination of much organisational effort by the people of Didsbury. The procession is seen here entering Didsbury Green from the direction of St Paul's, circling the Green and returning, probably on its way to Ford Bank. On the left can be seen a decorated wagon followed by a carriage. In the foreground — only just caught by the photographer — are decorated bassinettes, followed by girls (in fancy costume?). Just to the right of the lamp standard there are two photographers, their bulky plate cameras on tripods. The Wesleyan College is beyond the trees on the right, and the top of St Paul's church spire over the trees.

Didsbury Hotel, c.1900 *(above)*

The cabbies' shelter seeen here at the left was no longer required when horse-drawn cabs became obsolete. It had been both a shelter for the cab drivers and a store for horses' forage, but in the mid 1920's it was removed to Didsbury Recreation Ground. At about the same time the shelter from Didsbury Station was moved to the tram terminus at West Didsbury.

The arch at the left of the Didsbury Hotel allowed access for coaches, but has since been enclosed, although the footpath crossing can still be seen. Both the Didsbury Hotel and the Old Cock Inn advertised 'stabling', while the high wall beyond which is the roof of the Parish Church, enclosed the grounds of the old Parsonage (now Parsonage Gardens). At that time the gate into the Old Parsonage, where the garden wall is highest — immediately beyond The Cock — had not been built.

Ye Old Cock Inn, 1909 (right)

On the far left is the Eagle gateway, dated 1876 but not erected until 1902. The gateway gives access to the grounds of the Old Parsonage, and was originally a doorway from one of the old Spread Eagle hotels in Manchester. The street directories for 1871 to 1878 show six different pubs called The Spread Eagle in Manchester and Salford. None of them had been pulled down by 1876, but an earlier Spread Eagle in Long Millgate had been pulled down by 1869, and it is probable that the spread eagle and the gateway on which it stands came from this building. To the right of the archway is the access to the old stables and Wake Room — now demolished — of The Cock. The shop at the left survived, though not as a confectioners, until as recently as 1965, before being incorporated into the Inn.

The Old Parsonage, 1899 (below)

Fletcher Moss was a member of Withington Urban District Council from its formation in 1895, when Didsbury, Chorlton, Fallowfield, West Didsbury, Whalley Range and Withington were joined together to form this new local government unit. Half-way through its short life of ten years, this picture of members of the Council was taken in the grounds of Fletcher Moss's home, the Old Parsonage, now a branch gallery of the City Art Galleries and Museums.

The Old Parsonage's Kitchen Garden, 1909 (left)

At the beginning of the century, the ornamental gardens of the Old Parsonage were restricted to the area in front of the house, and were separated from this kitchen garden by a belt of trees and shrubs some of which can be seen here. Just to the right of the house is the conical 'swamp cypress' here about as tall as the house but now substantially taller. All the foreground is now laid out as grass with ornamental trees, and as herbaceous borders, so that this open view has been lost. The greenhouse seen here was replaced in 1987; the font which now stands close to the greenhouse entrance must be a post-1909 addition.

St James' Church, Didsbury, 1913 *(left)*

The church was built on or near to the site of what was probably the first chapel in the Parish of Manchester. (There were already two churches, one in Manchester and one at Ashton-under-Lyne).

Probably all the stonework visible today is early 17th century and later. There are stones just below the line of stringing over the north door in the tower which commemorate the extensive work of 1620. In 1801 more work was done and it was then that the decorative stonework at the top of the tower was added, replacing the seventeenth century work part of which was saved and used on the vestry extension on the south side. Through the trees to the right of the tower there is a view of the original Fernbank.

Didsbury Farm, Stenner Lane, c.1900 *(right)*

The foreground is now part of Fletcher Moss Gardens and Playing Fields. Of the buildings seen here only the Church and the farm building at the left, with double doors, survive. The house seen partly obscured by trees was the farmhouse, a much more substantial building than the row of cottages seen on the opposite page (top left) which were formerly almost opposite the door in the north side of the Church tower. The figure at the left is thought to be Mr Foulkes who farmed here in the early years of the century.

40

Stenner Brow (Spring Hill), Stenner Lane, c.1930

The gateway in the foreground is the Stenner Lane entrance to the Old Parsonage (now the Parsonage Gardens). The single-storey lodge — or Clerk's House — and the five cottages were demolished in about 1932, and the ground which they occupied incorporated into the Gardens.

Well Dressing in Stenner Lane, 1942 *(above right)*

Well-dressing was never a feature of Didsbury life before this century. It may have been introduced in about 1940. This is the lane-side of the farm building seen in the Didsbury Farm picture, and here a spring rises and feeds a trough in front of the building. The trough is still there, but covered over. Perhaps this wartime well-dressing scene is part of the drive for having Holidays at Home.

The Croft (now part of Fletcher Moss Gardens), 1917 *(right)*

This garden is part of the land given to Manchester Corporation by Fletcher Moss for use as a public park, although at the time of this picture it was still in private hands. The house is now used for tea rooms, shelter, and staff accommodation, and at first sight appears to be the building seen here. However, at some time in the past, the top storey was taken off and now the eaves are just above the line of decorative bricks, seen here as a dark line between the ground and first floor windows.

Millgate Lane (now Parrs Wood Road), November 1907 *(right)*

Millgate Lane Farmhouse, shown here, stood just south of the junction of Kingston Road and Millgate Lane. If today you stand on Parrs Wood Road, with Didsbury Lawn Tennis Club grounds on your left, you will see 513 and 515 Parrs Wood Road standing on the site of the farmhouse. The path through the stile led to Broadoak Farm and on to Didsbury Mill and it is still possible to follow the path to the site of the Mill, a journey which must have been undertaken twice a day by Mill employees, most of whom would live in Didsbury.

Wilmslow Road (East Didsbury)

1911 Coronation Festivities *(below)*

The corresponding car to that of the 1902 Festivities (see 639 Wilmslow Road picture), and probably the handiwork of the same person, can be seen here, this time in front of the Lodge of The Towers (now Shirley Institute etc.). Perhaps only the straw boater of the man leading the horse indicates the later date. The Boer War is still a strong memory, the Great War yet to come.

Construction of Kingsway, Parrs Wood, 1922

The former Midland Railway at Parrs Wood was almost at field level. In order to take Kingsway across the railway a ramp had to be built from School Lane southwards, and from Parrs Wood Lane northwards. In this picture preparatory work is in hand probably in connection with the construction of sewers. The track in the foreground is for the railed steam crane which was an essential feature of all such work. The bridle road linking School Lane Farm with Burnage Lane runs alongside the fence on the far side of the railway, and the buildings at the right are those of Bolton Wood Gate Farm at the south end of Burnage Lane. The field is the 'Round Meadow' of the Tithe Map, and the line of darker trees left of centre are in 'Burnage Lane Field'.

Didsbury Mill, c.1880 *(left)*

This water-powered corn mill was on a riverbank site, just beyond the south end of what is now Merston Drive, on the north bank of the Mersey, at the point where there was a weir and a mill-race. Although there is a reference to a mill at Didsbury as early as 1280, the one seen here is the 1820 building. It appears from the Rate Book to have been operational until 1885, when the Rate Book entry is marked 'Empty', and the rates are unpaid. Fletcher Moss writing in 1890 regretted that this historic building could not be put back into use. A new purchaser — the Rate Book shows 'James Watts' as the owner in 1890 — had announced his intention of refurbishing the mill to again use water power, and to erect a bridge over the river to give access to the railway, but threats of legal action from owners upstream, concerned about interference with drainage if the weir were to be rebuilt, caused the project to fail. The arch through which the millstream flowed can be seen at the left-hand end of the building. The mill was pulled down in 1959.

Turnpike Toll Bar, Wilmslow Road, Parrs Wood Lane, c.1882 *(right)*

The Turnpike Road from Wilmslow to Didsbury is the broad road curving to the left, with the side-gate from Parrs Wood Lane joining from the right, between the posts. The gatekeeper's house stood on the site which was until recently the entrance to the former Parrs Wood Bus Depot (demolished — apart from the clock tower — in 1988). The land behind the wall on the right is now the small garden in the triangle formed by Kingsway, Wilmslow Road, and Parrs Wood Lane.

The Turnpike Trust terminated on 1st November 1881, and the picture appears to show the position shortly afterwards, with the Wilmslow Road toll gate left open and unmanned, and the Parrs Wood Lane gate removed, leaving only the posts. The milestone at the edge of the shadow on the wall was saved (at road widening?) and can still be seen at the left-hand side of the double-gate entrance to the Parsonage Gardens in Stenner Lane.

River Mersey in Flood, near Stenner Lane, 1910

There have been artificial banks along the Mersey for hundreds of years and mostly they have been sufficient to prevent the river overflowing on to agricultural land. The last flood caused by the river overflowing was probably in 1965, since which time the Mersey & Weaver River Authority, whose duty it is to ensure the free flow of water down the river, have changed the nature of the river so that it almost has the appearance of a well-kept canal. At the same time they have strengthened the river banks, and so the combination of a more controlled flow of water together with stronger banks has probably put an end to flooding. In this view the tower of Didsbury Parish Church can be seen, with the spire of St Paul's Methodist Church to its left. The large, light-coloured house to the right is High Bank.

Red Bank Farm, c.1900 (*left*)

The farm buildings of Red Bank Farm, is shown, with the farmhouse itself almost hidden behind the trees at the right. The site of the farm is now the south end of Borrowdale Crescent (off Darley Avenue), the land on the left of the river being now part of Northenden Golf Club. The boundary between Didsbury and Northenden ran round the edge of the farm buildings so that, in this picture, the right-hand river bank was in Didsbury, but the farm buildings themselves were just in Northenden.